Through your own Eyes

David Agar and Kenneth Agar

Oxford University Press 1986

Oxford University Press, Walton Street, Oxford OX2 6DP

Oxford New York Toronto
Delhi Bombay Calcutta Madras Karachi
Petaling Jaya Singapore Hong Kong Tokyo
Nairobi Dar es Salaam Cape Town
Melbourne Auckland

and associated companies in
Beirut Berlin Ibadan Nicosia

Oxford is a trade mark of Oxford University Press

© Oxford University Press 1986

ISBN 0 19 911107 3

Set by Graphicraft Typesetters Ltd, Hong Kong
Printed in Hong Kong

Contents

All photographs are by David Agar

1 Giant Fern

Talking points

1 Say what you think is unusual or intriguing about this picture.
2 What could the man be pointing at?
3 As he points at the fern, what might the man be saying to his companion? Here are some suggestions:
   a 'Look how big that fern has grown. It was quite small when we passed it just now.'
   b 'Did you see that? Something looked out, then ran back in again.'
   c 'Is that someone's foot sticking out from under those fronds?'
   d 'Don't go near there! I heard a hissing sound.'
   e 'They say it grows in the rain forests and eats birds.'
   f 'How about one like that for our front garden?'

Which suggestion is *a*) the most likely; *b*) the most interesting; *c*) the most unbelievable?

Writing

Take one of the suggestions above or invent one of your own to write a conversation between the two people.

Drama/group work

Develop the conversation you have written into a play script. You can bring in other characters if you wish. Your scene could be comic, horrific, or scientific. In groups, act out your scene.

Vocabulary

creep slither rise grope seize expand
stretch spread sprout overrun runner
tendril root creeper entwine

2 The Storyteller

Talking points

1 Where might the man and child be sitting?
2 What could they be looking at?
3 What time of day and year do you think it might be?
4 What clues in the picture helped you decide?
5 Can you suggest what the relationship between the man and the child might be?

Writing

Imagine you are the man in the photograph and *either*:

1 You are telling the child a story. This may be an adventure story of places you once visited, or an imaginary tale of shipwreck and seamonsters, or something entirely different. Write your story.

Or:

2 The girl has spotted something which she has never seen before and is puzzled. Explain to her what it is she can see. Your description can be real or fantastic.

Vocabulary

oceans lagoons creeks waterfalls mountains
canyons peaks valleys plains prairies
liner tanker trawler horizon shipwreck

3 Cat Rescue

Talking points

1 What is the man doing? Here are some ideas:
   a He is trying to steal the cat.
   b The cat has jumped down to the window box below and he is trying to recapture it.
   c He is feeding the cat for his downstairs neighbour who is on holiday.
   Can you think of any other explanations?
2 Describe what might have happened after the picture was taken.
3 Can you think of any other instances of cats in peculiar or difficult situations?
4 People often take dangerous risks to help animals in difficulties. What do you think of this?

Group discussion

What are the problems of keeping pets in flats and other homes which have no access to a garden? Should pets be banned in such homes or should facilities be provided for them? Suggest what these could be.

Writing

1 In your home all pets are banned. However you have managed to smuggle in an animal of some kind and are keeping it in secret. Write a story about your relationship with your pet creature and the adventures you have with it.

2 Cats are well-known for their curiosity and habit of getting into difficult or dangerous situations. Write an account of 'A Day in a Cat's Life', describing its feelings as well as its encounters. You may use the scene in the picture, or invent one of your own.

Vocabulary

stranded abandoned ignorance compassion
affection protection objection indignation
nourish survive relieve extricate

4 The Arm

Talking points

1 What is peculiar about this picture?
2 What is the arm doing?
3 How is the arm able to work through the window of the door?
4 Why are all the blinds down?
5 Why is the window being cleaned from the inside instead of from the outside?
6 Who does the arm belong to? Suggest what the person looks like.

Drama/group work

Make up a scene in which somebody calls at the house and sees the arm. This could be a friend, a stranger, the police, or someone else. How does the visitor react? With surprise, amusement, bewilderment, fear, or shock?

Writing

Imagine you are the visitor who sees the arm. Invent a conversation with a neighbour or a passer-by telling them what you have seen, describing your feelings and telling them what you did.

Vocabulary

odd strange queer curious comic absurd extraordinary uncanny bizarre petrified mysterious perplexing disturbing illusion

5 Reflections

Talking points

1 How old is the man in the photograph? Can you tell?
2 What work is he likely to do?
3 What may he be carrying in his bag?
4 How do you know he is in a busy part of the town?
5 Is the man about to meet himself? If so:
   – what will he say to himself?
   – what questions will he ask?
   – what will he do next?
6 When you suddenly catch a glimpse of yourself in a window or a mirror:
   – how do you feel?
   – what do you think?
   – do you *say* anything?

Pair work/drama

1 Make up a conversation between the man in the picture and his double when they meet. One may be surprised and perhaps frightened. The other cool and calm, and perhaps threatening.

2 Mime the scene of a person reflected in a window or a mirror. One takes the part of the real person, the other the reflected image. You will need to plan and practise your moves first to give a convincing performance.

Writing

Write a story that begins: 'As I turned the corner I came face to face with a person who resembled me in every detail. We stared at each other in amazement . . .'.

Before you begin, decide how the story will develop. Will your mirror image become a real person like you or is it an illusion? Does the situation suggest a comedy, a hoax, or a crime? Who gets the blame for it all — you or your double?

Vocabulary

image mirror resemblance likeness
counterpart similarity duplicate control
merge combine supplant

6 At the Races

Talking points

1 Many different kinds of people go to the races for different reasons. Look at the pictures and see how many different kinds of people you can see. What are their reasons for being there?
2 How would you describe the people betting: foolish, greedy, daring, or optimistic?
3 How would you describe the atmosphere conveyed by the pictures?
4 Imagine you are at the races: what sounds and smells would you experience?
5 Which do you prefer: to attend a sporting event, or to see it on TV?
6 What are the advantages/disadvantages associated with each?

Group work

Make up commentaries on the race given by: a person with a large bet on a horse, one of the jockeys, a bookmaker, a TV sports commentator.

Writing

1 Select one of the photographs. Give it a caption and write an article to go with it for a newspaper or magazine.
2 Write a story entitled 'How I won the Derby'. This may be from the point of view of the horse, the jockey, the horse's owner or trainer, or maybe a spectator who places a winning bet.

A

B

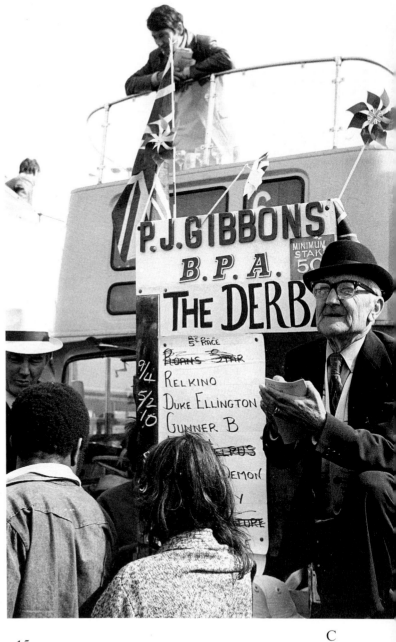

C

7 A Matter of Size

Talking points

1 What do the photographs have in common?
2 What helps you to decide the size of the different objects in the photographs?
3 Which is the most difficult to judge?
4 Which do you find the strangest photograph? Explain why.
5 If the pictures were stills from a film, what sort of story might it be?

Writing

1 The top picture is being used in an advertising campaign. Decide on the product it will be used to promote, and write an advertisement to go with it.

2 Imagine a situation in which you are suddenly much bigger or much smaller than your surroundings. Write a description of what you see and how you feel in this strange environment. In particular think about buildings and landscape, animals and people.

Vocabulary

miniature diminutive dwarf minute towering
gigantic massive mighty monument statue
megalith colossus

A

B

A

B

8 Visiting the Past

Talking points

Picture A

1 How can you tell this picture was taken outside a museum?
2 Do museums always look like this?
3 Look at the expressions on the faces of the children and their teacher. Can you imagine their thoughts and feelings?

Picture B

4 Can you work out what the man is looking at?
5 Do you think this was part of a larger statue? If so, can you imagine how large the whole thing might have been?
6 Why are statues often made 'larger than life'?
7 How does looking at something much bigger than yourself make you feel?

8 What do you find most interesting about looking at objects from the past?
9 What kind of things do you most like to see in a museum?

Group work/discussion

Discuss ways in which a museum can help with school studies. Do you think museums could do more to make visits by school pupils more interesting?

Writing

You are in charge of a new museum just opened in your area. What exhibits of special interest for your town or area would you include? What activities would you provide for school pupils? Write a description of how you would arrange and present the collections.

Vocabulary

displays galleries pottery sculpture
paintings statue effigy ruler image
memory prehistoric Greek Roman
medieval Egyptian

9 Dials and Switches

Talking points

1 This photograph shows a control panel. What do you think the panel is for?
2 Where might this picture have been taken? Here are some ideas:
   a in an ocean-liner
   b in a power station
   c in a space-rocket
   d in a computer room
   e inside the cockpit of a giant jumbo-jet.

   Which suggestion do you find *a*) the most likely; *b*) the least likely; *c*) the most interesting?

3 How did the boy get in there?
4 Is he doing anything dangerous?
5 Does he expect to make anything happen?

6 What other kinds of levers, switches and dials can you think of?
7 Why is it often tempting to want to operate the switches, levers and wheels of machinery?

Writing

Take one of the alternatives suggested above or make-up your own, and either invent a character or put yourself in charge of this control panel. How do you use your power and what happens as a result? Write your story.

Vocabulary

dial gauge scale pointer switchboard circuit fuse dynamo energy pressure nuclear hydroelectric

10 Sunday Market

Talking points

1 What sort of market is this?
2 Is there anything unusual in the mixture of items on display?
3 What is the boy on the left peering at?
4 Are the boys likely to know much about the goods on their stall?
5 What would you be interested in looking for at such a market?
6 Why do some people prefer shopping in this sort of market to shops?
7 Is it easy to get a bargain in a market or do customers have to haggle?
8 Describe a market like this you have visited and anything you or your family bought there.

Drama/group work

Set up a market scene with shoppers and stall-keepers. Make the characters as varied as you can. Act a scene in which suddenly one of the stall-keepers notices that something valuable is missing from his/her stall.

Writing

1 Using a market as the scene, take the part of a stall-owner, a policeman/woman, an onlooker, or a thief, and write a story entitled 'Theft'.

2 If you could be a market stall-keeper, what would you sell? How would you make your business successful? Write a description of your stall and the qualities needed to be a market-trader.

Vocabulary

antiques   curios   trinkets   bric-a-brac
Victoriana   interesting   valuable   beautiful
delicate   gaudy   decorative   unique   striking
novelty   rare

11 A Dog's Life

Talking points

1 Look at the dogs in the photographs. How would you describe their expressions?
2 Some people think that dogs and their owners tend to resemble each other. Is there an example of this in any of the pictures? Describe any instances you have seen.
3 Does any picture seem particularly British?
4 How would you describe the owner's treatment of his/her dog/s in each picture?

5 Every year many dogs are found abandoned. Can you explain how or why this happens?
6 Why do people keep dogs? Try and think of as many different reasons as you can. Are some reasons better than others?

Pair work

There are many different breeds of dog. Make a list of five breeds and for each one consider the following points:
– appearance
– easy or difficult to train and manage
– exercise: lots or little
– appetite: huge or moderate
– temperament: fierce or friendly
– busy streets: behaves well or badly

Which dog would best suit *a*) an old age pensioner; *b*) a disabled person; *c*) a family with young children; *d*) a farmer; *e*) you?

Writing

If a dog was allowed to choose its owner what sort of person would it prefer? Male or female? Rich or poor? Town or country dweller? Some dogs might want to be pampered, petted and spoilt while others would opt for a rough, tough existence. And some would want to work for their living. Write an account of 'How I Chose My Owner' by a particular breed or type of dog.

Vocabulary

kind compassionate humane generous intelligent faithful obedient trustworthy fierce ferocious retrieve reward

A

B

C

12 Crowd Scene

Talking points

1 What could the crowd be gathered for? Suggest what may be going on.
2 Look at the people in the crowd. Who is paying most attention to what is happening?
3 Who appears to be with a friend?
4 What is the young boy looking at?
5 Which of the people looks: happy, amused, indifferent, surprised?
6 How would you describe the young man on the right?
7 What is he carrying?
8 What may be his thoughts and feelings as he stands at the scene?

Pair work

Either choose two of the people in the picture and invent a conversation between them. *Or*, each choose a person in the picture, and describe this person to your partner. Can your partner identify the person from your description?

Writing

1 Choose one of the people in the picture and write a brief biographical description. Include as many details as you like to imagine, such as the person's age, name, family, background, home, work and character.

2 What is the young man on the right doing? Where has he been and where is he going next? Is he meeting someone, going home, going out with someone or doing something on his own? Taking the events in the photograph as a starting point, continue with a description of how he spends the rest of the day.

3 Write a story or poem entitled 'Crowds'.

Vocabulary

youngster youth teenager student pensioner housewife workman. technician unemployed anxious confident independent

13 Hat Trick

Talking points

1 Where might these pictures have been taken?
2 Suggest what the people are looking for.
3 Is the top hat for sale or is it being used for another purpose? If so, what?
4 What is interesting or unusual about the dummy?
5 What kind of face has it got: is it comic or serious, frightening or friendly, smiling or frowning?
6 Why has a necklace been put round its neck? Is there anything odd about this?
7 Does the head suggest any kind of riddle or mystery?

Writing

1 Imagine the kind of person the dummy might be modelled on. How does he spend his time? Where does he live and who does he know? Write a short story called 'A Day in the Life of . . .'.

2 Write a mystery/suspense story in which the dummy plays a central role. What is its secret? What part does the necklace and top hat play? Do any of the people in the pictures get involved?

Vocabulary

jewellery trinkets baubles symbol
memorabilia precious gems trader
merchant dealer angry scornful
determined haughty superior

14   What's Going On?

Talking points

1 Describe what the people are watching.
2 Why is there such a good audience?
3 The woman in the act was a volunteer from the crowd. Can you imagine how she felt when she realized what she was expected to do?
4 What use may be made in the act of the objects on the ground?
5 Why is the photograph more effective from this view-point than if it had been taken at ground level?
6 Describe any other examples of street entertainment that you can think of.
7 What particular attraction is there in open-air entertainment? What are the disadvantages?

Writing

1 Select three spectators in the crowd: perhaps a man, a woman and another gymnast. Write a separate paragraph by each in which the person gives a brief comment on the performance, saying whether it was skilful, entertaining or unusual.

2 You are a street entertainer of some kind. Decide what it is you do, and write a description of a typical day in your life. Consider how other people — such as the public, your family, the police, or other street performers — react to you and your work. Is it an easy existence or is it tough?

Vocabulary

dive vault hand-spring somersault balance support demonstrate strength agile nimble strenuous enterprising spectator impressive perform applause

15 Portraits

These are a group of portraits taken of an actor who was being considered for different roles in a play.

Talking points

1 Choose two contrasting pictures. What does each show about:
   – the sort of person the man is?
   – the sort of actor he is?
2 Take each of your pictures in turn and decide what acting role would probably suit him best.
3 Look again at all the portraits. Which picture shows the sitter's pose to be: friendly, thoughtful, worried, annoyed, puzzled?
4 Which picture do you think might be most liked by: his mother, his father, his wife, his children, his manager, himself?

5 What do you like or dislike about having your own portrait taken?
6 What is the most important aim of a portrait? Should it make the sitter look: natural, attractive, happy, intelligent, youthful or something else?
7 Do most people have their portrait taken for themselves, or for other people?
8 What helps a sitter to make a good portrait — good looks, self-confidence, being a good actor?
9 What sort of person makes the best portrait photographer?

Writing

The man in the photographs is missing and the police are searching for him. Say why he is wanted. Write details of his height, build, colour of eyes, hair and type of complexion. Describe any other identifying marks or ways of recognizing him which cannot be shown in the photographs. Say where he lived, the work he did and where he was last seen.

Vocabulary

slight   wiry   muscular   stocky   burly
lank   straight   unruly   moustache   beard
dark   pale   suave   dapper   well-groomed

16 Pavement Artist

Talking points

1 What is the artist using to make the picture?
2 Do you think it will be a good picture when it is finished?
3 Describe the effect of the eyes in the portrait.
4 Why do some artists decide to make their pictures on a pavement?
5 What is the fascination of watching an artist at work?
6 Can you think of any problems or difficulties that a pavement artist might face?
7 Why don't they display pictures they have made at home or in a studio?
8 What sort of living do you think they make?
9 What might they say about the high prices paid for some works of art?

Group work

How many different kinds of pictures do you see in the streets? In some towns the walls of old buildings and play areas are decorated with large pictures or designs. Hoardings and buses carry colourful advertisements. Are these examples of street art? Discuss whether such pictures improve the appearance of towns or if they should be controlled in any way.

Writing

1 Imagine you are looking through the eyes of the person in the incomplete portrait. Does the artist come back and finish drawing you? Perhaps you are then able to come to life and walk out of the picture. Or maybe it starts to rain.... Write an account of your thoughts and feelings as you watch the world go by.

2 Write a story about a pavement artist who becomes famous after a passer-by insists on buying the paving stones with the portrait on them.

Vocabulary

gaze   intense   compulsive   life-like   style
depict   tones   blend   recognition   praise
critic   review   temporary   transitory
priceless   worthless

A

B

17 Pilgrimages

PILGRIM: One who journeys to sacred place as act of religious devotion. (*Concise Oxford Dictionary*)

Talking points

1 What may be the reason for the gathering in each picture?
2 What do you think each group of people is hoping to do?
3 Are the people likely to have come from far to take part in each event?
4 Describe what you imagine are the feelings of the people in the pictures.
5 Look carefully at the pictures. What common shape appears in each one? Has this any significance do you think?
6 What is the strongest link between the two photographs?
7 Can you explain the title?

8 Can you think of any other present-day examples of 'pilgrimages'?

Writing

1 Either choose one of the pictures or think up your own example of a 'pilgrimage'. Write a notice from the organiser of the event, inviting people to take part. The notice should emphasise the importance of the meeting and the need for as much support as possible.

2 Write a sign or banner that a 'pilgrim' might carry. The message might be an ancient or a modern one. It could be an invitation, a warning, or a mystery.

Vocabulary

journey spiritual· hallowed crusade Christian doctrine belief holy festival vigil fellowship fraternity unite congregate quest

18 Bicycles

Talking points

1 Suggest at what time of day and year the pictures were taken.
2 What sort of day is it: windy, wet, dry, sunny, warm, cold, wintery, hot?
3 What could the cyclists be planning in the first picture?
4 What is happening in the second photograph?
5 What is likely to happen next?

6 What precautions should a group of cyclists take when travelling together?
7 Is it a good idea for cyclists to wear helmets or other protective clothing?
8 Describe the places in your locality which are most suitable for cycling.

Group work

Discuss cyclists and road safety. Should there be more laws to enforce road safety for cyclists? Some towns have cycle lanes marked out on the roads; should more of these be provided? Perhaps a publicity campaign to increase motorists' awareness of cyclists would also help.

How does a scheme like Cycling Proficiency Training help, and can it be improved?

Writing/designing a poster

1 You and your friends decide to start a school cycling club. Write a notice inviting other cyclists interested in joining. Decide on a title and make a list of the advantages of cycling as an enjoyable activity. These could include how cycling provides inexpensive transport, the freedom from time-tables, healthy exercise, the interest of visiting and exploring places and the skills it develops in map reading and planning journeys.

Give details of the type and condition of the bicycle each prospective member should own.

End by giving suggestions for some short and longer journeys to places that could be visited by the club.

2 Design a poster which is part of a cycling and road safety campaign. If you do not wish to draw it, describe the kind of picture you would use, and write the wording to go with it.

19   The Trees on the Hill

Talking points

1 How many people can you see in the picture?
2 Where would you expect to see trees like this: in a public park, open country, a private estate, or the grounds of a ruined castle?
3 What would you expect to find on the other side of the hill? Here are some ideas:
 – a wide plain
 – a deep valley
 – a high cliff
 – the sea
4 Estimate how old the trees are: twenty, fifty, a hundred, or more than a hundred years old?
5 What feelings do the trees suggest to you through their shapes, their size and their position?
6 Is there anything strange or sinister about any of them? What could you imagine about them?
7 Give the picture a title.

Pair work

When the boy on the right reaches the top of the hill, both his friends have vanished. While looking for them, he meets a stranger who tells him that the hill and the trees have a mysterious history.

Improvise a conversation between the stranger and the boy.

Writing

Write a story entitled 'The Legend of the Hill Trees'. Perhaps this could explain what has happened to the missing friends.

Vocabulary

towering immense soaring gigantic colossal
silhouettes look-outs defenders

20 Lone Horse

Talking points

1 What particular feeling does the picture give you — loneliness, adventure, mystery? Explain the reasons for your feeling.
2 Is it most likely to be dawn or dusk, winter or spring?
3 Do you think the picture was taken in Britain or another country?
4 Where has the horse come from and where is it going?
5 Is the horse looking for somebody or something?
6 If a human appeared, what sort of person would he or she probably be?
7 If you had to answer a young child who asked, 'Is it a tiny horse?', what would you say?
8 What sounds and smells would you probably notice if you were there?
9 If you used this photograph to paint a picture, what additions would you make?
10 Give your picture a title.

Group work

Imagine the horse is a runaway from a racing stable. Make up a radio interview with members of the stable who describe how they have been trying — without success — to recapture the horse.

Writing

1 Write a poem or story called 'Runaway'.
2 Imagine this photograph is for a book jacket. Decide what kind of book it is for, give it a title, and write the blurb to go on the back cover.

Vocabulary

Here are some descriptive phrases that might be useful:

curving hills empty sky ceaseless wind
solitary figure drumming hooves tossing mane
lonely tracks vast expanse

43

21 Watching and Waiting

Talking points

1 Have these people just arrived or have they been waiting for some time?
2 Where do you think they might be?
3 What or who could they be looking for?
4 What time of year do you think it is? What can you tell from their clothes and from the sky?
5 What is the mood of these people? Is anyone anxious, excited, bored — or something else?
6 Why is there a policeman and a dog?
7 What might happen next?
8 Write a caption for the photograph.

Pair work

Make up a conversation between any two of the people in the photograph. The dialogue should reveal the character of each person speaking and give an indication of the speaker's feelings, whether of curiosity, anxiety, calmness, boredom, excitement or whatever you choose to explore.

Writing

1 Choose one of the people. Describe from that person's point of view what he or she sees and express the feelings being experienced. Develop your description into a story about the scene which you imagine may be taking place.

2 Imagine the photograph is a still from a TV serial. Decide what kind of serial it is, and write an outline of the episode in which this shot appeared. You need to think about what happened the week before, and how the storyline will develop next week.

22 The Wave

Talking points

1 Can you tell in which order these pictures were taken?
2 Imagine you are on the beach. Describe the sounds and smells you would experience.
3 Why is it unlikely that pictures like these would be used to advertise the place as a holiday resort?
4 How could the pictures be used as a warning?
5 What safety precautions should a coastal town provide to prevent accidents during rough seas?

Pair work

Invent a telephone conversation about the rough seas between the local coastguard and one of the following:

a The skipper of a local fishing boat.
b The organizer of a yachting club which had planned a race for that day.
c A lifeboat which had answered a distress call from a ship but had failed to find it.

Writing/designing a poster

1 Design a poster warning the public of the dangers of rough seas, whether they are sightseers or amateur sailors.

2 Write a description or poem entitled 'The Wave'. Describe how it grows, approaches and breaks upon the shore, rises and then subsides.

Vocabulary

surf foam froth breakers billows shingle
burst fling explode bombard thunder roar
deafening hissing hurling drenching boiling

A

B

23 A Day Out

Talking points

1 What sort of place is each group of people visiting?
2 How interested are they in their surroundings?
3 Are the children being given much attention?
4 Who is enjoying the day out most, the children or the adults?

Picture A
5 Why is the man looking in the opposite direction to the child and the woman?
6 What else have they been doing that day? Are there any clues?

Picture B
7 What might be the relationship of the two women to the girl?
8 What might the girl be looking at through the binoculars?

9 On a family outing, what sort of place best caters for everybody's interests?
10 Describe the most interesting or the most boring place you have visited with your family.

Group work/in threes

Choose one of the pictures and make up a dialogue which might be taking place. Each take the role of the child or one of the adults in each group. There may be long silences, isolated comments, bored responses, and interruptions. Make the conversation as realistic as you can.

Writing

1 Choose one of the pictures and write a dialogue between the adults, which is interrupted by the spoken thoughts of the child.

2 Write a story or description of the most interesting, or the most boring, day out you have ever spent. Your writing may be based on fact or fantasy.

Vocabulary

recreation   refreshments   crowds   amusements
admission   surroundings   displays   prohibit
manners   Sunday-best   behaviour   politeness

24 On the Bridge

Talking points

1 Suggest in which month of the year this picture was taken and describe the day.
2 How would you describe the people's expressions?
3 Choose one of the people and give a more detailed description. Think about the person's age, occupation, and what thoughts he or she may have while walking across the bridge.
4 What are the people watching? Is something happening on the river?

Group discussion/drama

Imagine this is a scene from a TV series or film. What could this be about? Here are some suggestions:
– a romantic thriller
– a spy drama
– a story about drug-smuggling
– a 'whodunnit' mystery.

Pick one of these suggestions or make-up one of your own and cast each of the characters, inventing more if you wish. Then work out the events that have led up to this scene and what follows. The ending should suggest more to come rather than a conclusion. The bridge and the river are crucial to the action.

Act out your scene.

Writing

1 Make a list of the characters' names and the roles they play. Write a 'shooting script' for the scene to go on film. Use your own experience of viewing films or television to present the story in a way that will make it exciting. Give instructions for the camera operator to take shots from different distances and angles and to produce different movements. Give details of the sound effects that should be recorded.

2 How are you going to interest people in your film or series: what will encourage them to watch it? Design a leaflet or poster to publicize your work.

25 The Waiting Room

Talking points

1 In what sort of place do you imagine the station to be?
2 What feeling or mood does the picture give you?
3 Is the woman waiting to get on a train or to meet someone?
4 If she is to meet someone, suggest who it might be.
5 Imagine the woman's thoughts and feelings as she waits.
6 What other kinds of 'waiting room' are there?
7 Describe the feelings and mood you associate with each of them.

Group work/drama

1 The station waiting room begins to fill up. The train is heard approaching. What does the woman do? Does a visitor arrive? Or does something else happen? Act out a scene showing what happens when the train arrives.

2 Think of a 'waiting room' situation and act it out. Try and include as many different kinds of people as you can. How is each character likely to behave as they wait . . .?

Writing

1 Imagine that many years later the woman remembered the night she waited for the train. Write her account of what happened when the train arrived.

2 Write a TV sketch based on an incident in a waiting room: this could be dramatic, mysterious, exciting, or sad.

3 Write a poem which conveys the mood and atmosphere of the photograph.

26 The Travellers

Talking points

1 Give a detailed description of the photograph, looking closely at the landscape and the two figures.
2 Can you suggest what country it might be?
3 What mood or feeling does it give you?
4 Look again at the two figures and decide who they might be. Could they be related?
5 Suggest where they have come from and where they are going.
6 How would you describe their journey: dangerous, tiring, long, hot, or difficult?
7 Why are they walking instead of travelling by train?

Pair work

Decide on the relationship between the two people in the picture. Here are some suggestions:
– mother and daughter
– grandmother and grandchild
– neighbour and child
– aunt and niece.

Choose one of these or make-up one of your own, and invent a conversation between them.

Writing

1 Write an account of a close relationship between a young person and an adult: either the two people in the photograph, or you and an older member, or friend, of your family. Describe the effect each person has on the other.

2 Write a story or a poem suggested by the picture, entitled 'The Journey'.

Vocabulary

affection trust sympathy bond favourite
companion family gratitude protect
memories confide support encourage
guide instruct

A

B

27 The Musicians

Talking points

1 Why have the musicians chosen to play in each particular spot?
2 How are their surroundings likely to affect their choice of music and the way they play it?
3 Are they likely to be members of a group or band?
4 If so, suggest what they are called and describe the kind of music they play.
5 Suppose these two pictures are for a record sleeve. Give the record a title and describe the kind of music on the record.

6 Do surroundings affect your enjoyment of listening to music? What sort of places do you enjoy music in the most?
7 Can music influence your feelings about your surroundings? Describe any experiences you have had like this.
8 Do you prefer to hear 'live' music or music on records, tapes, or disks?
9 What are the advantages/disadvantages of each of these?

Drama

1 There is a freight train travelling on the line where the two men are playing. It pulls up a few yards from them and the driver gets out. Invent a scene with the musicians and the driver.

2 You are out at sea when suddenly you hear a faint noise on the breeze. It sounds like music, but you can't believe it can be. Act a scene in which the boat crew hears strange sounds and one of them spies the musician on the headland.

Writing

1 Write a lyric to go with the music you imagine any of the musicians are playing.

2 Describe your favourite piece of music and say where in the world you would most like to hear it played. Would you get the musician/s to play it for you, or would you prefer to hear it on your own music equipment?

Vocabulary

melody echoes reverberate clangour
crescendo harmony imitate reproduce
improvise create impulse imagination
inspired outraged irresponsible scale

A

B

28 Relics

Talking points

Picture A

1 What does this picture illustrate about some people's behaviour?
2 Do you find the car body in such a place strange, funny, or offensive?
3 Could the car body be used for anything else?

Picture B

4 Where did the clock face probably come from?
5 Why is it unlikely to be from a modern clock?
6 Why do you think the clock face has been dismantled?
7 What other use could it have now?

8 Do you find relics like these sad, ugly, amusing, or something else?
9 Describe any strange or interesting examples of 'relics' that you have seen.

Writing

1 Use each picture to write an imaginary notice or an advertisement. The notice could be a warning or a request. The advertisement might aim to publicize a product or a service in a light-hearted or amusing way.

2 Write a story or poem entitled 'The Relic'. Imagine what your relic was once like and compare it with its present state — broken, damaged, disused, discarded, forgotten. Try and build up mood and feeling in your writing.

Vocabulary

vehicle limousine saloon road-safety
timeless timekeeper timetable time-worn
abandoned dismantled discarded memorial

29 Staircase to Nowhere

Talking points

1 Why does the staircase not go to the top of the building?
2 What alteration would have to be made for it to be any use?
3 Suggest any uses that could be made of it in its present form.
4 Explain why you think this staircase was built.
5 Could the staircase be dangerous in any way?

6 Explain how a spiral staircase may be more convenient or more attractive than a straight one.
7 Does it matter if some things have no practical use?
8 What other 'useless additions' could be built on to a house?

Pair work/drama

1 Mime a slapstick scene in which a pair of comedians (such as Laurel and Hardy) try to make use of the staircase.

2 You are the owner of the house and come back from holiday to see this staircase has been built. You ring up the builder to try and find out what's going on. . . . Make-up your conversation.

Writing

1 Write a story in which the staircase plays a central role. Your tale could be comic, serious or horrific.

2 You are an estate agent trying to sell a house with a useless addition of some kind. Write a description, for your sales particulars, of the impractical extra. You may choose the house in the photograph, or think up another unusual building.

30 Mystery TV

Talking points

1 Does this picture say anything to you? Is it ridiculous, absurd, amusing, or outrageous?
2 Why is the screen empty do you think?
3 Why do you think the photographer chose to take this photograph? Is there a hidden message?

4 A kind of art which uses familiar objects in strange surroundings and dreamlike settings is called *surrealism*. Is this picture 'surreal' do you think?
5 What effect does a 'surreal' picture have on you?
6 Would you describe any other pictures in this book as 'surreal'?

Writing

Suppose the set has special powers. There are three channels: *a*) past; *b*) present; *c*) future.
Tune in to a time and place of your choice. Decide on:
– the period
– the place
– the people
– the events

Decide whether the plot is to be comic, frightening, or nonsensical, and write an outline for a short play or a documentary. Is the play to be short and complete or a series of episodes?

Vocabulary

vision image flicker fade dissolve
transmit project reception network monitor
unreal fantasy illusion convince deceive

31 Shadows

Talking points

1 Give an explanation – perhaps a fantastic one – as to where you think the people are.
2 Are most of the people young, middle-aged or old?
3 Why is one person not walking?
4 Which shadow looks: happy, fashionable, bored, interested?
5 Is it possible to guess anything about a person's character or appearance from his or her shadow?

6 In what ways do some shadows make a scene or a picture more interesting?
7 What do you dislike about some shadows?
8 In what ways are night-shadows different from shadows seen in daylight?

Group work

Take the part of any of the shadows in the picture. Make up a scene in which they meet and discuss their lives as shadows. Remember they can only exist in the light, — in sunlight, electric light, candlelight, or firelight for example.

Writing

Write a fantasy in which you find yourself in a place inhabited only by shadows. You find a way of communicating with them. What are the shadows: do they represent the thoughts of their owners or are they imaginary beings with an independent life? Do you escape from them or do you become a shadow too?

Vocabulary

appear re-appear disappear vanish dissolve
fade fleeting flicker dart materialize
blank void featureless profile transform

32 Figures at the Door

Talking points

1 What sort of building would have a doorway like this?
2 Is the building in a good state of repair?
3 What is interesting or unusual about the building?
4 Why is there a number and a letter box?
5 What are the two figures doing there?
6 Can you tell anything from their actions, or the way they dress?
7 Invent a name, an occupation, and a character for each.
8 Consider these alternatives:
  a The figure on the right is a ghost, a being with supernatural powers who can travel through space and time.
  b The 'ghost' is simply a trick produced by the photographer.

Which explanation do you find *a*) most interesting; *b*) most convincing?

Group work

Discuss the subject of the supernatural. What do you believe? Do ghosts exist, are they completely imaginary, or are you unsure? Give examples of what you have read about, seen, or imagined. Say why you think people are so interested in tales or accounts of the supernatural.

Writing

1 Imagine you are the photographer who was unaware of the 'ghost' until the photograph was developed. Write a story about your reaction to what you find.

2 Imagine the photograph is a still from a spooky film, originally taken from a novel or collection of short stories. Write the title and the descriptive blurb on the book jacket. Remember that blurbs should give a brief sketch of plot and character, but do not have to tell the whole story.

Vocabulary

spirit spectre poltergeist phantom
supernatural transparent float glide
materialize vanish eerie chill alarm
haunt avenge time-warp

33 Telephone Calls

Talking points

1 How would you describe the mood or feeling of these pictures?
2 Do you find them intriguing, mysterious, bizarre, or something else?
3 Suggest what may be going on in the sequence. Consider the following questions:
   a What may the phone calls be about?
   b What has happened in *Picture B*?
   c Why has the man left the telephone box in *Picture C* and where has he gone?
   d What is the woman doing, or about to do, in *Picture C*?
   e Has the child any significance? Who does it belong to?
   f Is the partly demolished building in the background important?
4 If there was a fourth photograph in the sequence, what might it show?

Pair work

Decide what the calls are about. Are they friendly chats, urgent messages, or requests for help? You could either take the part of the woman and her caller, or the man and his caller. Or maybe the man and the woman accidentally get connected to each other. Make up the conversation between the speakers.

Writing

Use the sequence of events in the photographs to write a short, three scene play for radio. Link the two people and the child so that they form part of one story. The ruined building should play an important part. Remember to include details of all sound effects.

Vocabulary

discussion   decision   understanding   disruption
broken   demolish   disagreement   advice
accommodation   destruction

34 Street Scene

Talking points

1 Which city do you think this street could be in?
2 Which features in the photograph helped you decide?
3 What feeling or mood does the picture convey?
4 Look at the building in the centre of this picture. What is strange or unusual about it? What might it be?
5 Who is the man standing outside this building? Why might he be standing there?
6 What about the other two men: are they strangers or friends? Are they having a disagreement, a quarrel, or simply a discussion?
7 Describe the girl sitting on the kerb. Consider her mood as well as her physical appearance. Why could she be sitting there and what might she be thinking?
8 Which of the people in the picture would you like to know more about? What would you like to know?

Drama/group work

Invent a scene with the people in the picture. Decide what has just happened before the picture was taken and what is going to happen in the future. Take up the same positions as the people in the picture — as the camera clicks the action begins.

Writing

1 Take one of the people in the picture and write a brief biographical description.
2 Write a description of this area of the city for someone who hasn't seen the photograph.
3 Imagine you are the photographer. Explain why you took the photograph. Say what you like about it. Describe what happened after you took it.

Vocabulary

up-market community rich cosmopolitan
seedy neighbourhood expensive depressed
fashionable bargain-hunter's paradise
dirty squalid confusion dispute

35 Stately Pigsty

Talking points

1 Describe the house in the background.
2 When do you think anybody last lived there?
3 What kind of house might it have been?
4 What has happened to it now?
5 What are the pigs doing there?
6 How do you feel about them being there?

7 Why has it become difficult for owners of large houses to live in them?
8 How do they try and overcome this problem?
9 Describe a stately home that you have visited. Did you find the visit interesting or not?

Group work

Imagine members of the local Council visit the house in order to report on whether it can be restored. Their guide is an elderly servant who once worked in the house.

Act a scene in which the group are shown some of the historical features. Finally they enter what was once the spacious dining room only to find it has been taken over by the pigs.

Writing

1 Imagine the owner of the house returns after a long absence to find that it is now a ruin and has been taken over by the pigs. Describe the scene facing the owner and his or her reactions to it.

2 The house can be used for whatever purpose you like. Describe the changes you would make to the house and say how it will be used in future.

Vocabulary

imposing heritage noble grand ancestral dignified west-wing parkland baronial hall aspect spacious disgrace shame humiliate insult scandal

36 Butcher's Shop

Talking points

1 Can you tell where this shop is most likely to be?
2 Why are the pigs heads on display?
3 How do they make you feel?
4 Why do people eat meat? Think of as many reasons as you can.
5 Some people live on meat-free diets. What sort of foods would you need to eat if you weren't eating meat?
6 Can you think of any problems in being a vegetarian?

Pair work

What is a healthy diet? Together draw up a list of the foods you think your body needs to stay healthy.

Now each make a list of the food and drink you have consumed within the last few days. How do your lists compare with your idea of a healthy diet? Do you think that either of you are eating too much of one kind of food and not enough of another?

Writing

1 Look at the picture closely, and then write down the first five words that come into your mind. Use each word to start a short sentence about the picture. Develop your sentences into either a piece of descriptive writing, or a poem entitled 'The Butcher's Shop'.

2 Design a poster persuading people to eat more meat, or more vegetables, depending on your viewpoint.

A

B

37 Trade Unions

Both photographs were taken during the same Trade Union march.

Talking points

1 Describe the mood of the marchers in each photograph.
2 What does NUPE stand for?
3 What type of work do members of NUPE do?
4 Why do you think the march is being held?
5 Why is the woman carrying a megaphone in *Picture B*?
6 Why are there children on the march?
7 What is the policeman doing on the march?

8 Are all Trade Union marches as peaceful as this?
9 Why do people belong to Trade Unions? Think of as many different reasons as you can.
10 Suppose the National Union of Students (NUS) extended its membership to include school students. How would you react?

Group work/discussion

You want to start a union, either for people of school-age who work part-time, or a student union in school. Think of as many different reasons as you can why you think it's necessary and a good idea.

Writing

1 Write a manifesto outlining the aims of your union and conditions of membership. How much will you charge people to join? Will there be a penalty for not joining? What are your rules about strikes? How do you hope to improve the working conditions of your members?

2 Your local council is proposing to make cuts in the bus-service. The drivers call a strike because they think the council could make savings in other ways.
   Write two letters to the local newspaper: one a letter of complaint at the hardship the strike is causing, the other a reply from one of the drivers, explaining why he or she is on strike.

A

B

38 The March for Jobs

In 1983 a 'march for jobs' was organized, when a large number of unemployed people marched from different parts of Britain to London to protest against the continuing lack of work.

Talking points

1 What sort of places is the march passing through in the pictures?
2 How do the marchers appear: cheerful, miserable, defiant, determined, or united?
3 What are the reactions of passers-by? And the police?
4 What do you think the demonstrators hope to gain from the march?
5 Upon whom do you think the march had the most effect?
6 Is going on a march an effective way of protesting about unemployment?
7 Apart from the need to earn a living, what are the most important aspects of having a job?
8 Why has there been so much unemployment in recent times?
9 In what ways can unemployed people create their own work? Are these effective?

Pair work

Take the part of a radio reporter and an unemployed marcher and conduct a five minute interview to be broadcast on radio. You will need to decide what aspects of the march to focus on. It could be that the reporter and the marcher will want to draw attention to different aspects of the march, so think carefully about how you are both going to achieve what you want to say.

Writing

1 Write an article that might appear in your local newspaper describing how a group of unemployed school-leavers decide to start their own business. Being untrained and without work experience they begin by offering simple services for which nothing organized exists at present. Describe what you imagine they offer, the problems they face and what success they eventually achieve.

2 'In the year 2086 . . .' Write a description of how you would like to see society in the future. How will people spend their time? Will there be work for everyone? Will people need to do the same kind of work as is done today?

Try to be as original and creative as you can.

79

39 Nuclear Disarmament

Talking points

1 Look at the expressions on the faces of the people in the photograph. Which of them looks: determined, curious, dedicated, angry, amused?
2 Why has one of the marchers dressed up as a waiter?
3 What specific point is he trying to put across?
4 Is he making his point effectively?
5 The membership of the Campaign for Nuclear Disarmament (CND) grew from 3,000 in 1979 to over 100,000 in 1985. What reasons can you think of for this increase?
6 What impression of CND is presented in the press and on radio and TV? Do you think your attitude to CND has been influenced by what you have read and seen?
7 Do you think that the possession of nuclear weapons makes a country more safe or not?
8 Do you think that protest campaigns like the Campaign for Nuclear Disarmament can have any effect on government policy?

Writing

You are a reporter for a local newspaper. Write an article describing the march and the effect it had upon the people in the different districts it passed through. Were there any demonstrations against it, did some people show approval and join in? Describe the mixture of people who took part. You can include 'interviews' with some of the marchers or passers-by if you wish. Try and keep your account factual and unbiased.

Project

Find out as much information as you can about Nuclear Defence and CND. Look out for newspaper articles, advertisements, government information on defence, and CND information.

Use your information to present a case either for or against nuclear disarmament.

81

40 The White Birds

The 'birds' in the photograph appeared one day in the streets around Westminster in London.

Talking points

1 What is your reaction to the birds? Do you find them intriguing, friendly, menacing, comic, or something else?
2 Explain how they might have been used to publicize something.
3 What kind of product or service could they be advertising?
4 Maybe they are connected with religion or politics in some way. What do you think?
5 Perhaps they are part of some sort of entertainment, or celebration, or carnival. If so, can you imagine what sort?

6 Describe any street processions or festivals you have seen or know about, in which outsize or grotesque creatures appear.

Group work/drama

Make up a scene in which the birds play a central part. Decide what the birds could represent – friendship, peace, hunger, poverty, or something else. Are they being used to influence people? Do they have a spokesperson, and what is the message? Is there disagreement and opposition from some of the spectators?

Writing

1 It is one hundred years from now, and this photograph has been found, but without any explanation as to the meaning or purpose of the birds.

Write an article as if you are an historian of those future times, in which you describe what you think the birds represented and the effect they had on the people who lived at the time of the photograph.

2 Write a story or poem entitled 'Carnival'.

41 Celebrations

Talking points

1 If you had been at the scene, what sounds would you have heard?
2 Where is this taking place?
3 Where are the men from do you think?
4 What are they celebrating?
5 Why are the police taking no notice?
6 Which of the following would you use to describe their behaviour: harmless high-spirits, irresponsible, juvenile, or boisterous?
7 What caption would you expect to see under the picture if it appeared in: a) The Sun; b) The Daily Telegraph; c) The Scotsman?
8 Should people be allowed to act like this?

Group work/drama

Act a scene between:
a An indignant passer-by and a police officer
b A police officer and two of the men
c One of the men and members of his family upon returning home.

Writing

1 Write a short newspaper report to accompany the picture.

2 Write what you think about the behaviour of some football supporters. First make a list of the points you want to mention, such as:
   – are reports exaggerated?
   – are most supporters well-behaved?
   – who causes the trouble, and why?
   – do pictures like this on TV encourage trouble?
   – how could you prevent violence?

Use a separate paragraph for each point. Make the final paragraph a summary of your opinions.

3 Why do you think there is more violence associated with football than with other sports?

Vocabulary

triumph defeat conquer vanquish rejoice supporter hooligan vandal riot brawl disorder precautions pacify control restrain prohibit exclude segregate cordon custody

42 Law and Order

Talking points

1 Suggest where this picture was taken.
2 What are the policemen doing there?
3 Describe how the policeman looking at his helmet probably feels.
4 What is the other policeman looking at?
5 What do you think the man with dark glasses is thinking?
6 Why do you think the photographer took this picture?

7 How do we react when we see something like this happen to someone else?
8 Would we react differently if the 'victim' were not in uniform?
9 What if it is someone we know: how do we react then?

Writing

1 Write a caption and a paragraph to go with the photograph if it were to appear in one of the daily newspapers.

2 What is the most embarrassing thing that has ever happened to you, or that you can imagine happening? Write a story entitled 'My most embarrassing moment'.

Vocabulary

target bulls-eye direct-hit missile
undignified accidental disrespect blemish
dismay consternation misfortune

43 River Patrol

Talking points

1 Suggest where this photograph might have been taken.
2 Where was the photographer standing when he took the picture?
3 What season of the year was it?
4 Can you tell what time of day it was?
5 What might the two policemen standing together be looking at, or waiting for?
6 Why do you think the third policeman is walking away?
7 Write a caption for the photograph.

8 Are the police concerned mainly with criminals and law breakers?
9 What kinds of events do the police attend? Why are they present?
10 Is police work different from what is often shown in TV plays or in films?

Group work/in threes

Make up a conversation between the three policemen when they were together *before* the photograph was taken.

Then make up the dialogue between the two left behind. You will have to decide what they were doing and why they were there.

Writing

1 Write up your dialogue into a play-script. Remember to include details of the scene, and stage directions. Give your play a title and decide at what point in the action this scene takes place.

2 Suppose you are on the committee that selects applicants for police training. What special skills and qualities do you look for in recruits to the police force?

Write a description of the sort of person who could make a good policeman/woman.

44 The Tree

Talking points

1 Where was the picture taken?
2 Why is there a question mark after 'un arbre'?
3 What kind of wall is it? Is it the wall of a building, a boundary wall, or have you any other ideas?
4 What do you imagine is taking place on the other side of the wall?
5 How important are the trees in the picture?
6 What are your feelings about this picture — despairing or hopeful?
7 In what way is the photograph a comment on the damage people do to the environment?
8 Is our environment threatened more seriously today than in the past? If so, in what ways?
9 What sort of graffiti might be seen on this wall if it were in Britain?

Pair work

Make up a conversation between the person who wrote the graffiti and a member of the French police who appears on the scene just as it is finished.

Writing/designing a poster

1 Write a poem entitled, 'The Last Tree'.

2 Friends of the Earth is an organization that tries to protect the natural environment from being damaged or destroyed by unsightly buildings or developments. Design a poster to publicize their work.

3 *Either*: 'Graffiti is a form of vandalism. It is written by thugs who have no respect for the environment.'
Or: 'Graffiti is an attempt by people to express their views and opinions on things that matter to them. It is a form of art.'
   Write an essay using either of these statements as a starting point. You should take care to think your opinions through, before writing.

A Final View

1 Select up to four of your favourite photographs from this book and say why you chose them.

2 Make a collection of interesting photographs from newspapers and magazines and any you have taken yourselves. Choose pictures which convey a particular mood or idea rather than sensational news pictures. Arrange these into a display and give each a caption.

3 'The camera never lies.' How true do you find this statement? Begin by reconsidering some of the photographs. For example, you could look at *The Arm* (p. 11), *Reflections* (p. 13), *Shadows* (p. 65), and *A Matter of Size* (p. 17).

4 What factors in a photograph create a particular feeling or atmosphere? Look again at *Lone Horse* (p. 43), *The Trees on the Hill* (p. 41), *The Waiting Room* (p. 53), and *On the Bridge* (p. 51). How has the photographer emphasised the mood of the picture? Can you tell anything from these about the attitude or character of the photographer?

5 Many of the photographs in the book could be stills from a film or TV series. Select several which could be from the same film or series and put them in sequence. Then give your film a title and write an outline of the story and characters involved.

6 The way we see a subject affects our feelings, our thoughts and the language we use in talking or writing about it. Has any picture in the book influenced you in forming and expressing an opinion? Give details.

7 This book includes both black and white and colour photographs. Is one type better than the other? Which subjects are best in which medium? Give examples from here and elsewhere to support your opinion.

8 Compare the moving pictures seen on television or film with still photographs. What are the advantages or disadvantages of each? Say which you prefer, give examples, and the reasons for your choice.

9 Some subjects may be more effective as paintings than as photographs. Look through the photographs and write some comments on which subjects you would prefer as paintings.

10 Photography was unknown before 1829. How might our knowledge of history be altered if photographs had been available? Suggest some subjects which would have made interesting photographs in showing the way people lived in the past.